Leckie
the education publisher
for Scotland

2nd Level Maths

2B

Practice Workbook 1

© 2024 Leckie

001/01082024

10 9 8 7 6 5 4 3 2 1

The authors assert their moral rights to be identified as the authors for
this work.

ISBN 9780008680350

Published by
Leckie
An imprint of HarperCollins Publishers
Westerhill Road, Bishopbriggs, Glasgow, G64 2QT

T: 0844 576 8126 F: 0844 576 8131
leckiescotland@harpercollins.co.uk www.leckiescotland.co.uk

HarperCollins Publishers
Macken House, 39/40 Mayor Street Upper, Dublin 1, D01 C9W8, Ireland

Publisher: Fiona McGlade

Special thanks
Project editor: Peter Dennis
Layout: Jouve
Proofreader: Julianna Dunn

A CIP Catalogue record for this book is available from the British Library.

Acknowledgements
Images © Shutterstock.com

Printed in India by Multivista Global Pvt. Ltd.

Contents

Answers
Check your answers to this workbook online: https://collins.co.uk/pages/scottish-primary-maths

1.1 Rounding whole numbers to the nearest 10, 100, 1000

1 Complete the boxes:

Write the multiple of 10 that comes either side of each number.		
6630	**6632**	6640
	6642	
	6652	

Write the multiple of 100 that comes either side of each number.		
6600	**6632**	6700
	6732	
	6832	

Write the multiple of 1000 that comes either side of each number.		
6000	**6632**	7000
	7632	

2 Rounding up or rounding down.

Draw an ⬆ or ⬇ beside each number to show if it rounds up or down.

a) 7824 to the nearest 10

b) 7824 to the nearest 100

c) 7824 to the nearest 1000

d) 5055 to the nearest 10

e) 5055 to the nearest 100

f) 5055 to the nearest 1000

3 Have these numbers been rounded to the nearest 10, 100 or 1000? Tick the correct box.

			10	100	1000
61 452	→	61 000			✔
61 452	→	61 450			
61 442	→	61 400			
61 444	→	61 440			
61 944	→	62 000			

⭐ **Challenge**

Think of a four-digit number that rounds up when it is rounded to the nearest 10, rounds down when it is rounded to the nearest 100 and rounds up when it is rounded to the nearest 1000. How many answers can you find?

1.2 Rounding decimal fractions to two places

1 Write or circle the number in the correct place on these number lines.

7·43
```
7·0   7·1   7·2   7·3   7·4   7·5   7·6   7·7   7·8   7·9   8·0
```

7·43
```
7·4   7·41  7·42  7·43  7·44  7·45  7·46  7·47  7·48  7·49  7·5
```

7·53
```
7·0   7·1   7·2   7·3   7·4   7·5   7·6   7·7   7·8   7·9   8·0
```

7·53
```
7·5   7·51  7·52  7·53  7·54  7·55  7·56  7·57  7·58  7·59  7·6
```

7·63
```
7·0   7·1   7·2   7·3   7·4   7·5   7·6   7·7   7·8   7·9   8·0
```

7·63
```
7·6   7·61  7·62  7·63  7·64  7·65  7·66  7·67  7·68  7·69  7·7
```

2 a) Write each decimal fraction in the correct column if they are rounded to the nearest whole number.

4·67   4·57   4·37   3·47   3·57   5·27

Rounds to 3	Rounds to 4	Rounds to 5	Rounds to 6

b) Fill in any empty boxes with numbers of your own.

3

Please mark my work. Put a circle around any I have to correct.

Starting number	Nearest tenth	Nearest whole number
3·62	3·6	4
14·05	14·0	14
27·79	27·8	28
0·81	0·8	0
75·08	75·8	76
49·36	49·3	49

★ **Challenge**

Use the digits below to make decimal fractions with three digits that round to 5 when rounded to the nearest whole number. Each digit can be used only once.

| 0 | 1 | 2 | 3 | 4 | 5 | 6 | 7 | 8 | 9 | 4 | 5 | · | · | · | · |

Is there only one way to do this?

1 Use rounding to help you estimate an answer. Match these calculations to the most reasonable estimate.

33 + 59	100	31 + 59
37 + 59	90	35 + 59
159 − 31	130	159 − 33
159 − 35	120	159 − 37

2 Round the prices on the shopping list to see if Finlay has enough money.

I got £10 for my birthday and I am spending it on these.

Chocolate	£ 1·49
Comic	£ 3·99
Pencils	£ 1·12
Bath toy	£ 3·55

Explain your answer.

3 Complete the table.

	Rounded to nearest thousand	Estimated answer	Rounded to nearest ten	Estimated answer
5982 + 2012	6000 + 2000	8000	5980 + 2010	7990
5982 + 3012				
5982 − 4012				

4 Use rounding to estimate each answer. Write the estimate in the correct column.

	More than 2500	Less than 2500
4631 – 1892		
4031 – 1892		
4631 – 1092		
4631 – 1992		
1992 + 1992		
1992 + 2092		
1992 + 2492		
1992 + 2692		

★ **Challenge**

Isla is at the book shop. She sees two books that cost more than £3 each. She estimates that the two books will cost £7·90. What might the price of each book be? How many answers can you find?

2.1 Reading and writing whole numbers

1 Write these numbers in the place value houses using digits.

a)

Thousands			Ones		
T	O		H	T	O

Thirty-three thousand and three

b)

Thousands			Ones		
T	O		H	T	O

Thirty-three thousand and thirty

c)

Thousands			Ones		
T	O		H	T	O

Thirty-three thousand, three hundred

d)

Thousands			Ones		
T	O		H	T	O

Thirty-three thousand, three hundred and three

2 Write these numbers in words.

a)

Thousands			Ones		
T	O		H	T	O
5	9		0	5	9

b)

Thousands			Ones		
T	O		H	T	O
5	0		9	5	0

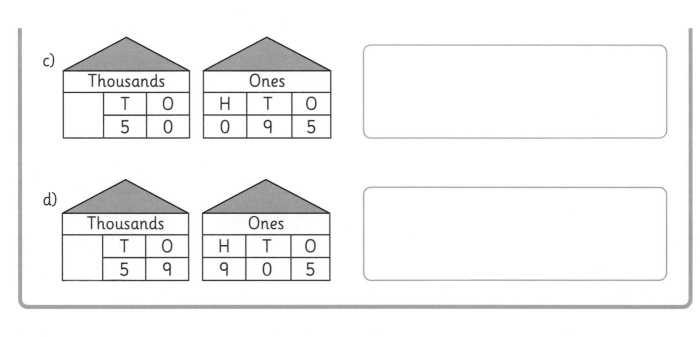

c)

Thousands		Ones		
T	O	H	T	O
5	0	0	9	5

d)

Thousands		Ones		
T	O	H	T	O
5	9	9	0	5

3 Read these numbers aloud. Mark in each time you say 'and'. The first one has been done for you.

67 5⌃72   67 000   67 500   67 540   67 543   67 503

What do you notice?

★ Challenge

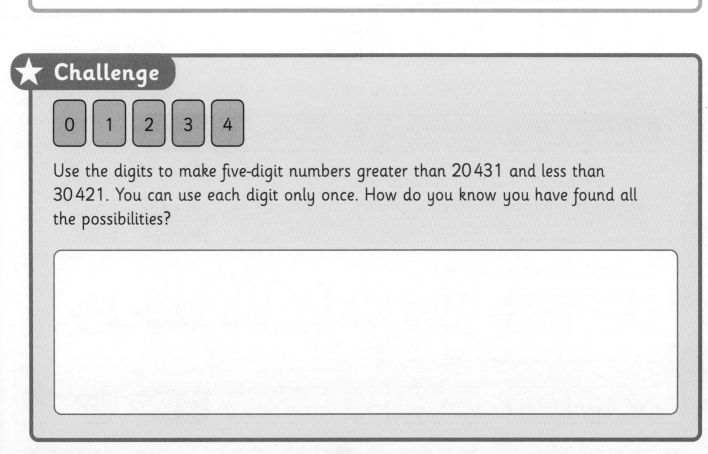

| 0 | 1 | 2 | 3 | 4 |

Use the digits to make five-digit numbers greater than 20 431 and less than 30 421. You can use each digit only once. How do you know you have found all the possibilities?

2.2 Representing and describing whole numbers

1 Write a five-digit number where the digit 3 has the following value:

3 ones or 3

3 tens or 30

3 hundreds or 300

3 thousands or 3000

3 tens of thousands or 30 000

2 Write the correct digits onto the place arrow cards to show each number.

a) Five thousand, six hundred and thirty

b) Eighty-five thousand, six hundred and thirty

c) Eighty-five thousand, three hundred and six

d) Eighty-five thousand and thirty-six

e) Eighty thousand and sixty

3 Complete the Think Board for the number 61043.

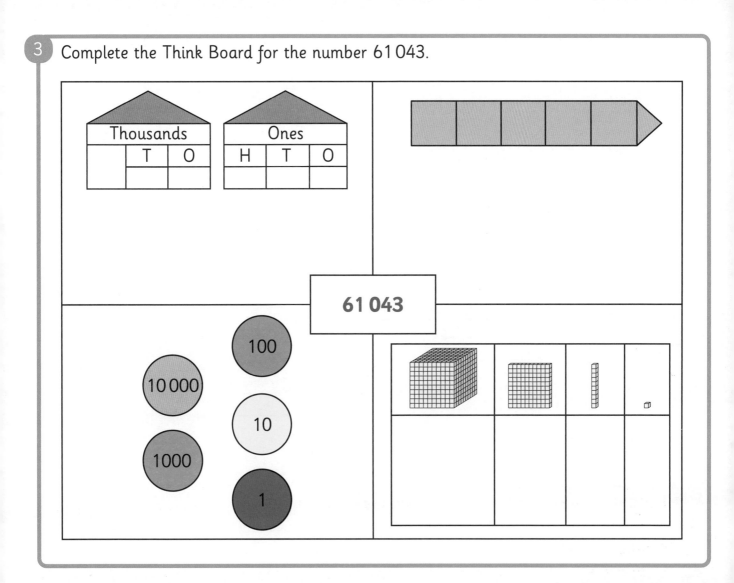

⭐ **Challenge**

0 1 2 3 4 5

Using the digit cards 0 to 5 find as many as possible five-digit numbers between 34520 and 40532 that fits both criteria:

• are even numbers

• hundreds digit is greater than the thousands digit.

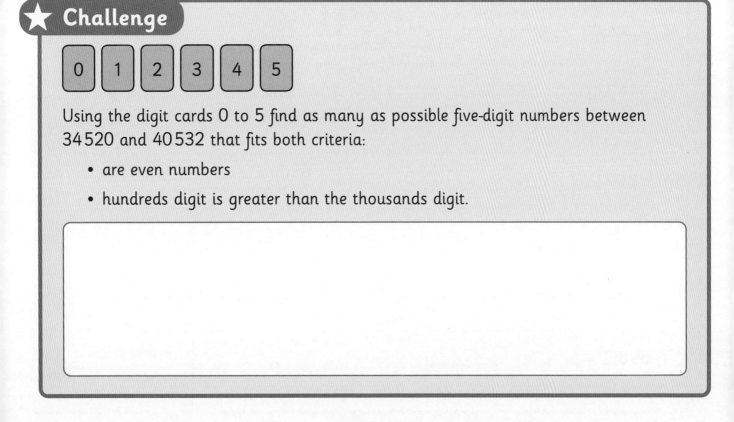

2.3 Place value partitioning of whole numbers

1 Tick the statements that show correct partitions. Correct any wrong answers.

a) $5670 = 5000 + 600 + 70$

b) $7979 = 7000 + 97 + 9$

c) $34\,612 = 30\,000 + 4000 + 600 + 2$

d) $62\,523 = 60\,000 + 2000 + 500 + 20 + 3$

2 Partition these numbers One has been done for you.

a) $23\,875 = 20\,000 + 3000 + 800 + 70 + 5$

b) $89\,560 =$

c) $54\,602 =$

d) $78\,021 =$

e) $60\,532 =$

f) $60\,050 =$

3 Complete the table. What is the bold digit worth? One is done for you.

6**6**666		6000			
66666					
6666**6**					
666**6**6					
66**6**66					

4 What number is shown here? Fill in the first column. One is done for you.

13579	10000	3000	500	70	9
	10000	4000	500	70	9
	10000	4000	400	70	9
	10000	4000	400	80	9
	10000	4000	400		9

5. Complete the table. Can you find four different ways to make these numbers? Fill in the blanks.

	Thousands	Hundreds	tens	ones
		14		
1465				65
	1			
			146	
		25		
2576				76
	2			
			257	
		36		
3687				87
	3			
			368	

You will need a dice.

1. Roll the dice and choose one square to fill in. Keep rolling the dice and filling in a square every time.

   - Try to make Nuria have the greatest number.
   - Try to make Finlay have the lowest number.
   - Try to make Amman be closest to 25 000.
   - Try to make Isla be closest to 30 000.

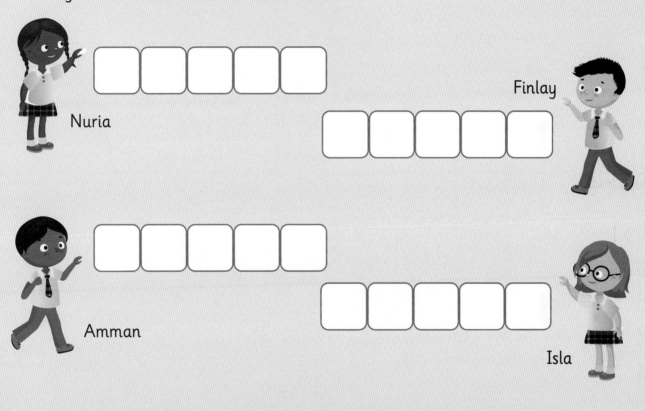

Nuria

Finlay

Amman

Isla

2. Write about how well your final numbers fit the rules.

1 Keep the sequences going by counting in 10s.

a) 30, 40, _____, _____, _____, _____, _____, _____

b) 37, 47, _____, _____, _____, _____, _____, _____

c) 237, 247, _____, _____, _____, _____, _____, _____

d) 307, 297, _____, _____, _____, _____, _____, _____

e) 1307, 1297, _____, _____, _____, _____, _____, _____

2 Complete the blanks.

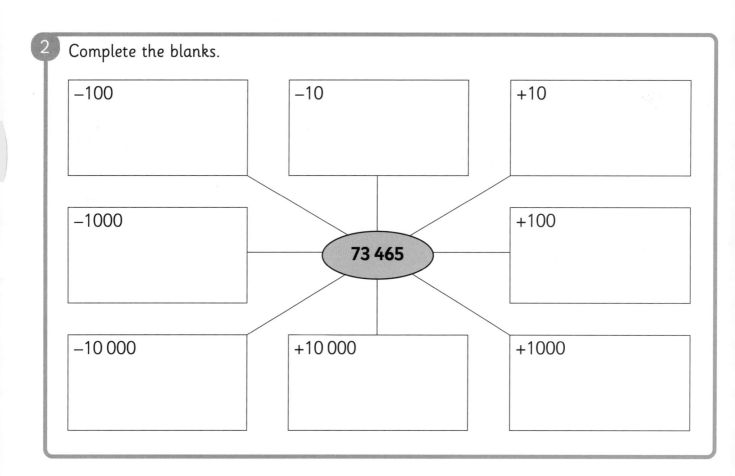

−100

−10

+10

−1000

73 465

+100

−10 000

+10 000

+1000

3 Work out these number sentences:

a) 38 890 + 10 = [ ]

b) 38 990 + 10 = [ ]

c) 38 890 + 100 = [ ]

d) 38 990 + 100 = [ ]

e) 38 890 + 1000 = [ ]

f) 39 990 + 1000 = [ ]

4 What has been added or subtracted to these numbers to make them balance? One has been done for you.

a) 24 506 → 24 406 [– 100]

b) 34 506 → 34 606 [ ]

c) 34 506 → 34 406 [ ]

d) 34 506 → 33 506 [ ]

e) 34 506 → 34 496 [ ]

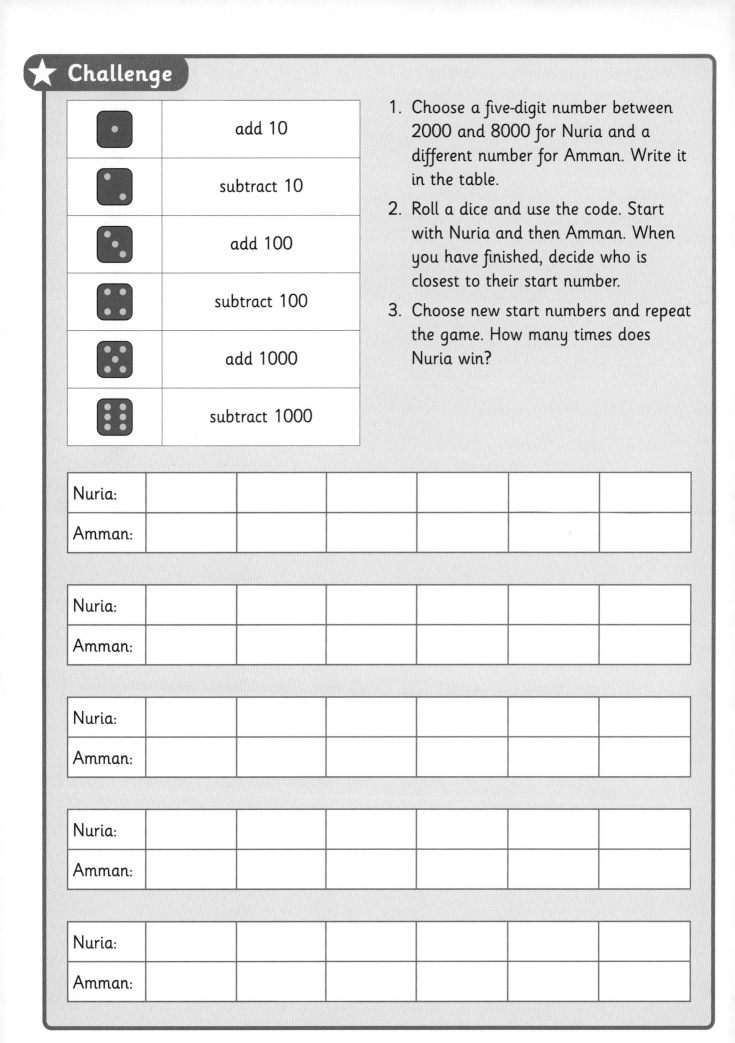	add 10
	subtract 10
	add 100
	subtract 100
	add 1000
	subtract 1000

1. Choose a five-digit number between 2000 and 8000 for Nuria and a different number for Amman. Write it in the table.

2. Roll a dice and use the code. Start with Nuria and then Amman. When you have finished, decide who is closest to their start number.

3. Choose new start numbers and repeat the game. How many times does Nuria win?

Nuria:						
Amman:						

Nuria:						
Amman:						

Nuria:						
Amman:						

Nuria:						
Amman:						

Nuria:						
Amman:						

1 Write the number that the first digit is worth in each of these. One has been done for you.

a) 65 000 ➤ 60 000

b) 650 ➤ _____

c) 6500 ➤ _____

d) 5600 ➤ _____

e) 56 000 ➤ _____

Now put the answers in order from smallest to largest.

_____ _____ _____

_____ _____

2 Complete these statements using < or >.

a) 21 087 ☐ 21 097

b) 21 087 ☐ 21 084

c) 21 187 ☐ 20 087

d) 21 087 ☐ 20 987

e) 21 087 ☐ 21 807

f) 20 087 ☐ 20 870

3 The table shows spectators at football matches on one Sunday in May.

Team	Spectators
Glenfield United	4845
Hillside Albion	40845
Riverdale F.C.	4895
Shore United	1845
Rockvalley F.C.	14805
Woodburn City	20895

a) Write the names of the teams in order from largest numbers of spectators to smallest.

b) What is the difference between the smallest and largest crowd numbers?

4 Complete these to make them true.

a) 34 506 > | 3 | 4 | | | 6 |

b) 34 506 > | 3 | | | 0 | 6 |

c) 34 506 < | | | 5 | 0 | 6 |

d) | 3 | | | | 6 | < 30 606

e) | 3 | | | | 6 | > 39 006

★ **Challenge**

Use the digits 0 – 9 to make the statements true. You can only use the digits once. How many different ways can you do it?

| 0 | 1 | 2 | 3 | 4 | 5 | 6 | 7 | 8 | 9 |

| | | | | | < 81 605

| | | | | | > 19 495

1

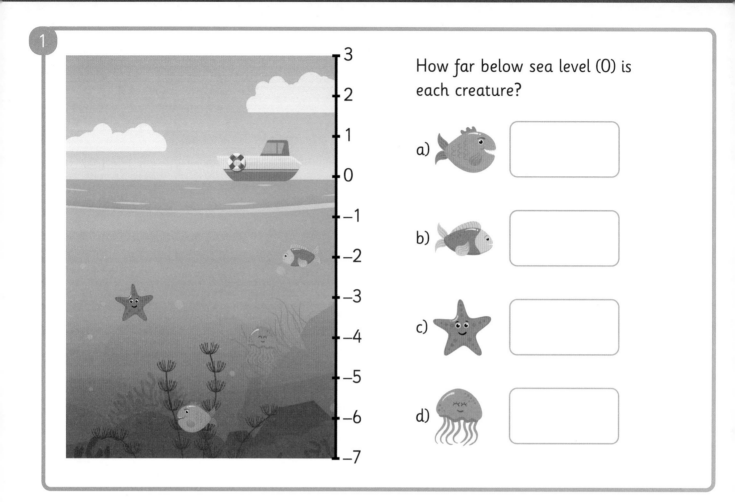

How far below sea level (0) is each creature?

a) [ ]

b) [ ]

c) [ ]

d) [ ]

2 Look at these temperatures. Circle the temperature which is colder.

a) 10°C or 12°C

b) 0°C or 2°C

c) −2°C or 0°C

d) −12°C or 10°C

e) −49°C or −19°C

f) 49°C or 19°C

g) −49°C or 19°C

h) 49°C or −19°C

3 Keep these sequences going.

a) 4, 3, 2, 1, 0, –1, _____ , _____ , _____ , _____

b) 40, 30, 20 _____ , _____ , _____ , _____ , _____

c) –7, –6, _____ , _____ , _____ , _____ , _____ , _____

d) –70, –60, _____ , _____ , _____ , _____ , _____

4 Use < or > to make these statements true.

a) –6 ☐ –7

b) –6 ☐ 7

c) 6 ☐ –7

d) 0 ☐ –7

e) –6 ☐ 0

f) –60 ☐ –70

★ **Challenge**

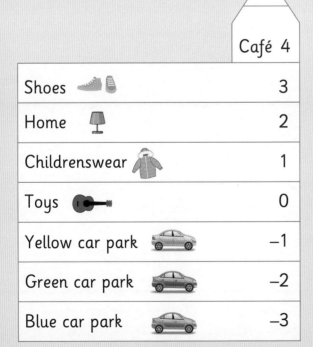

Café	4
Shoes	3
Home	2
Childrenswear	1
Toys	0
Yellow car park	–1
Green car park	–2
Blue car park	–3

Amman takes the lift in the shopping centre and goes up three floors. Write four possible lift journeys where he might have started and then got out of the lift.

25

2.7 Reading and writing decimal fractions

1　a) What decimal fraction does each diagram show?

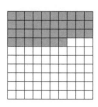　　　　　　　　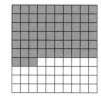

b) Colour the diagrams to show the following decimal fractions.

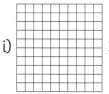　　Show 0·31

　　Show 1·31

　　Show 1·03

2　Circle the odd one out:

a) 9·06　　nine point six　　$9\frac{6}{100}$　　b) 9·6　　nine point six　　$9\frac{6}{100}$

c) 9·61　　nine point one　　$9\frac{61}{100}$　　d) 6·09　　six point nine　　$6\frac{9}{100}$

e) 6·99　　six point ninety-nine　　$6\frac{9}{100}$

3 Complete the table.

Words	Diagram	Decimal fraction	Mixed number
One point seven five			
			$2\frac{55}{100}$

★ Challenge

What number does each child have?

My number has 6 tenths and 5 hundredths.

My number has 3 more tenths and 4 more hundredths than Amman.

My number has 5 more hundredths than Amman.

My number has 7 more tenths than Amman.

2.8 Representing and describing decimal fractions

1 Colour the grids four different ways to show 0·45.

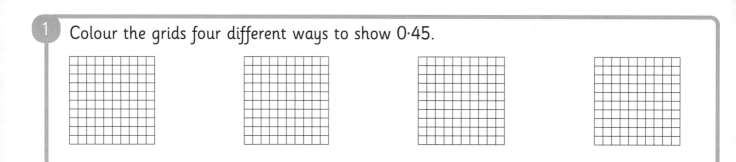

2 Complete the table. The first one is done for you.

Diagram	Decimal fraction (shaded part)	Decimal fraction (unshaded part)	Fraction (shaded part)
	0·25	0·75	$\frac{25}{100}$

3 Match the decimal fraction to the fraction.

a)   1·34 $1\frac{30}{100}$

b)   1·04 $1\frac{4}{100}$

c)   1·3 $1\frac{34}{100}$

d)   34·1 $34\frac{10}{100}$

e)   34·01 $34\frac{1}{100}$

★ Challenge

How many different numbers can you make using these place value arrows? You can use 1, 2 or 3 arrows each time.

| 6 > | 0·3 > | 0·08 > |
| 2 > | 0·7 > | 0·04 > |

1 Write these decimal fractions in the grid below. Think about where each number can go.

Write them from largest to smallest.

9·06   9·86   36·69   13·8   9·65   9·6   24·17

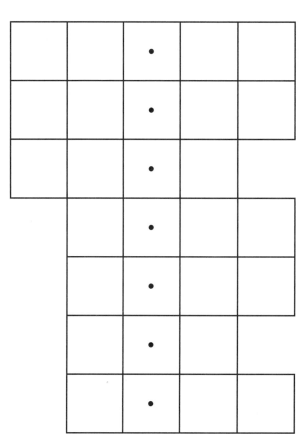

2 Use the symbols =, < or > to compare these decimal fractions.

a) 27·17 ☐ 27·19

b) 27·07 ☐ 20·77

c) 15·45 ☐ 15·55

d) 15·5 ☐ 15·05

e) 60·9 ☐ 6·95

f) 60·90 ☐ 60·9

3 Write the numbers from largest to smallest.

a) 0·1   0·15   0·01   _____ _____ _____

b) 1·67   1·7   1·77   _____ _____ _____

c) 28·04   28   28·4   _____ _____ _____

d) 0·50   5·0   0·05   _____ _____ _____

e) 4   4·1   4·01   _____ _____ _____

★ Challenge

1. For each decimal number, roll a dice and write a number into one of the empty boxes. Keep rolling and filling in the empty boxes. Can you make six numbers that are all less than 60?

a) [ ][ ] · [ ][ ]   b) [ ][ ] · [ ][ ]

c) [ ][ ] · [ ][ ]   d) [ ][ ] · [ ][ ]

e) [ ][ ] · [ ][ ]   f) [ ][ ] · [ ][ ]

2. List your numbers from smallest to largest.

[   ]

3. Try again but this time try to make all the numbers less than 30.

a) [ ][ ] · [ ][ ]   b) [ ][ ] · [ ][ ]

c) [ ][ ] · [ ][ ]   d) [ ][ ] · [ ][ ]

e) [ ][ ] · [ ][ ]   f) [ ][ ] · [ ][ ]

3.1 Mental addition and subtraction

1 Calculate the following:

a) 156 – 30 = [ ]

b) 136 + 30 = [ ]

c) 687 – 120 = [ ]

d) 567 + 120 = [ ]

e) 503 – 40 = [ ]

f) 503 + 40 = [ ]

g) 758 + 70 = [ ]

h) 758 – 70 = [ ]

2 Transform these calculations. Two have been done for you.

a) 134 + 159 = [133 + 160]

b) 144 + 149 = [ ]

c) 698 + 36 = [ ]

d) 697 + 136 = [ ]

e) 159 – 42 = [160 – 43]

f) 158 – 62 = [ ]

g) 477 – 139 = [ ]

h) 809 – 49 = [ ]

3 Transform these numbers and calculate mentally. Jot down numbers that help.
The first one is done for you.

607 + 269 606 + 270 806 + 70 876	607 + 267	499 – 46	499 – 48
698 + 146	696 + 148	701 – 54	703 – 54

⭐ **Challenge**

You are only allowed to use the digits 8, 9 and 0 for this challenge. Create a four-digit plus three-digit sum. Transform and solve the question.

[0] [8] [9]

[ ] [ ] [9] [ ] + [ ] [ ] [ ]

= [ ] [ ] [ ] [0] + [ ] [ ] [ ]

= [ ] [ ] [ ] [ ]

3.2 Adding and subtracting a string of numbers

1 Circle the numbers in each question which total a multiple of 100. One has been done for you.

Space for jottings

a) (4550) + 3423 + (150)

b) 3460 + 1240 + 3016

c) 230 + 3044 + 3070

d) 1580 + 1520 + 1582

e) 710 + 5602 + 490

2 Circle the numbers which total a multiple of 10 or 100 and calculate mentally. Jot down numbers if it helps. The first one is done for you.

Space for jottings

a) 6523 – (179) – (221) = | 6123 |

b) 6523 – 189 – 211 = | |

c) 6803 – 189 – 211 = | |

d) 6803 – 355 – 245 = | |

e) 6803 – 155 – 145 = | |

3 Look for multiples of 10, 100 or 1000. Calculate mentally and jot down numbers to help.

(670) + 1026 + (230) =
1026 + 900
1926

5740 – 290 – 410 =

6522 – 2500 – 1500 =

7604 + 196 + 177 =

1045 – 307 – 23 =

644 + 466 + 156 =

★ Challenge

1. Write pairs of numbers that help you add or subtract these calculations mentally. Can you find different pairs that help? The first one has been done for you.

   a) **934 + 766 + 104**   766 + 104 = 870   34 + 66 = 100

   b) 547 + 1453 + 107

   c) 2006 + 1994 + 594

2. Now create two additions of your own with numbers that total multiples of 10 or 100 in them.

35

1 Partition each number into its place values. The first one is done for you.

a) 14 567 ➜ 14 000 + 500 + 60 + 7

b) 14 507 ➜

c) 15 067 ➜

d) 15 007 ➜

e) 15 670 ➜

2 Use partitioning to work these out. Look at the example first.

21 342 + 4526 ➜ 21 000 + 300 + 40 + 2 + 4000 + 500 + 20 + 6 ➜
25 000 + 800 + 60 + 8 = 25 868

a) 10 546 + 2522

b) 10 546 + 354

c) 454 + 20 546

d) 20 546 − 445

e) 20 566 − 556

3 Use place value to calculate:

a) 36 278 + 4321

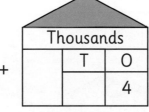

Thousands			Ones		
T	O	H	T	O
3	6	2	7	8

+

Thousands			Ones		
T	O	H	T	O
	4	3	2	1

Thousands			Ones		
T	O	H	T	O
4	0	5	9	9

36 thousands + 4 thousands equals 40 thousands

2 hundreds + 3 hundreds equals 5 hundreds

7 tens add 2 tens equals 9 tens

8 ones and 1 one equals 9 ones

b) 40599 – 4321

Thousands		Ones		
T	O	H	T	O
4	0	5	9	9

–

Thousands		Ones		
T	O	H	T	O
	4	3	2	1

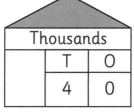

Thousands		Ones		
T	O	H	T	O

c) 40599 – 5421

Thousands		Ones		
T	O	H	T	O
4	0	5	9	9

–

Thousands		Ones		
T	O	H	T	O
	5	4	2	1

Thousands		Ones		
T	O	H	T	O

d) 5491 + 23 218

Thousands			Ones			
	T	O		H	T	O
		5		4	9	1

+

Thousands			Ones			
	T	O		H	T	O
	2	3		2	1	8

Thousands			Ones			
	T	O		H	T	O

⭐ **Challenge**

Fill in the blanks to make the statement true.

1 ☐ 3 2 ☐ + ☐ ☐ 5 5 = 2 4 6 ☐ 6

8 0 ☐ 9 8 − 1 ☐ 4 ☐ 4 = 6 ☐ 3 5 4

3.4 Using place value partitioning

1 Add these numbers by partitioning. The first one is done for you. Remember to line up your columns.

a)
```
    3  4  4  2  3
 +  1  2  5  7  2
────────────────
    4  0  0  0  0
       6  0  0  0
          9  0  0
             9  0
                5
────────────────
    4  7  9  9  5
```

b)
```
    3  4  4  2  3
 +  1  2  5  2  7
────────────────
```

c)
```
    3  4  4  3  3
 +  1  6  5  2  7
────────────────
```

d)
```
    1  6  5  2  7
 +  3  4  5  2  7
────────────────
```

2 Subtract these numbers by partitioning. The first one is done for you.

a)

		7	8	6	3	7
	−	6	5	5	1	4
		1	0	0	0	0
			3	0	0	0
				1	0	0
					2	0
						3
		1	3	1	2	3

b)

		7	8	6	3	7
	−	5	5	5	2	4

c)

		7	8	6	3	7
	−	3	5	5	3	4

d)

		7	8	6	3	7
	−	3	5	6	2	7

41

3 Use partitioning to calculate the following:

a) | 8 | 6 | 6 | 5 | 7 | – | 7 | 5 | 4 | 4 | 4

b) | 7 | 6 | 5 | 4 | 6 | – | 6 | 5 | 4 | 4 | 4

c) | 5 | 1 | 0 | 2 | + | 6 | 4 | 9 | 1 | 8

d) | 6 | 4 | 9 | 0 | 8 | + | 5 | 1 | 0 | 2

Fill in the missing numbers to make each calculation correct.

a)

	7	2	8	6	3
−	☐	☐	☐	☐	☐
	5	1	1	3	3

b)

	7	2	8	6	3
+	☐	☐	☐	☐	
	7	8	9	9	7

★ Challenge

Choose from the following numbers to create an addition calculation. Write the partitions out like the calculation in question 1 and work out what your starting numbers are.

+

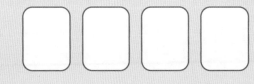

6000   20 000

10   70

7   1000

500   2

1 Complete the following sentences. The first has been done for you.

a) 26 + 5 = 2 tens + 6 ones + 5 ones. This is 2 tens + 1 ten + 1 one.

b) 46 + 7 = 4 tens + 6 ones + 7 ones.

This is

c) 460 + 70 = 4 hundreds + 6 tens + 7 tens.

This is

d) 460 + 74 = 4 hundreds + 6 tens + 7 tens + 4 ones.

This is

e) 740 + 46 = 7 hundreds + 4 tens + 4 tens + 6 ones.

This is

f) 46 + 74 = 4 tens + 6 ones + 7 tens + 4 ones.

This is

g) 460 + 730 = 4 hundreds + 6 tens + 7 hundreds + 3 tens.

This is

2 Use column addition to work these out.

a)
```
  4 3 5 6
+ 2 3 2 7
---------
```

b)
```
  4 3 5 6
+ 2 3 7 2
---------
```

c)
```
  4 3 5 6
+ 2 7 3 2
---------
```

d)
```
  4 3 5 6
+ 7 2 3 2
---------
```

e)
```
  1 0 0 6
  4 5 0 6
+    5 0
---------
```

f)
```
  2 0 0 6
  3 5 0 6
+   5 0 0
---------
```

g)
```
  2 5 0 6
  3 5 0 6
+       5
---------
```

h)
```
  2 5 6 0
  2 0 6 0
+ 5 0 0 0
---------
```

3 Use column addition to work these out.

a) 6207 + 544 + 291

b) 654 + 201 + 6217

c) 7328 + 312 + 65

★ **Challenge**

The answer is 1368.

1 2 3 4 5 6 7 8 9

1. Use the digits 1 to 9 to create an addition calculation that gives this answer. You can only use each digit once.

2. Use the digits 1–9 to create a different addition calculation that gives this answer. You can only use each digit once.

+

+

1   3   6   8

1   3   6   8

3. Can you find more possible answers?

45

1 Complete the calculations. The first one is done for you. You could use a different coloured pencil to show your negative numbers.

a)
```
    7 1 6
  - 3 4 2
    4 0 0
  -   3 0
        4
    3 7 4
```

b)
```
    7 7 1
  - 2 3 4
  _____

  _____
```

c)
```
    5 0 8
  - 1 7 4
  _____

  _____
```

d)
```
    9 4 0
  - 5 3 7
  _____

  _____
```

2

Check my answers and tick them if they are correct.

a)
```
    8 0 8
  - 5 9 5
    3 0 0
  -   1 0
        3
    3 1 3
```

b)
```
    7 0 7
  - 4 9 5
    3 0 0
  -   9 0
        2
    2 1 2
```

c)
```
    6 8 0
  - 1 0 4
    5 0 0
  -   8 0
        6
    4 2 6
```

d)
```
    5 8 0
  - 2 2 9
    3 0 0
      6 0
  -     9
    2 3 9
```

e)
```
    5 8 0
  - 1 9 3
    4 0 0
  -   1 0
  -     3
    3 8 7
```

3 Use the space below to do Isla's corrections from question 2.

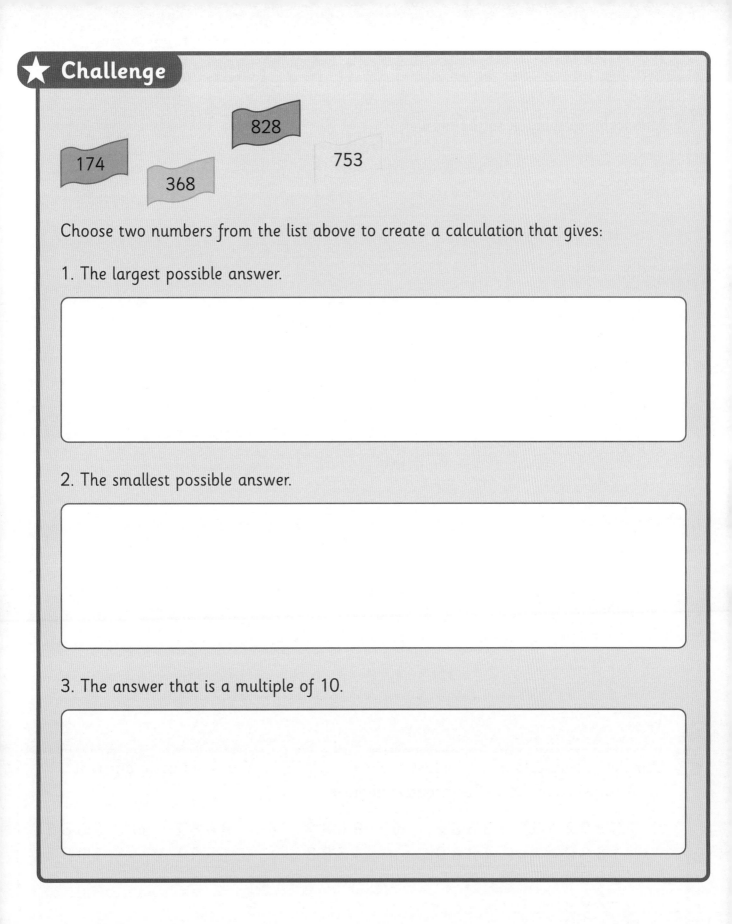

828

174

368

753

Choose two numbers from the list above to create a calculation that gives:

1. The largest possible answer.

2. The smallest possible answer.

3. The answer that is a multiple of 10.

1 Match the calculation to the answer.

a) 600 – 400

b) 900 – 500

200

c) 700 – 500

300

d) 800 – 400

e) 600 – 300

400

f) 800 – 500

2 Complete the calculations. The first one is done for you. You could use a different coloured pencil to show your negative numbers.

a)
```
    3 6 9 2
  – 1 8 8 0
  ─────────
    2 0 0 0
    – 2 0 0
        1 0
         2
  ─────────
    1 8 1 2
```

b)
```
    3 6 8 2
  – 1 8 8 0
  ─────────

  ─────────
```

c)
```
    3 6 8 2
  – 1 5 8 8
  ─────────

  ─────────
```

d)
```
    8 6 8 2
  – 1 5 9 1
  ─────────

  ─────────
```

e)
```
    8 6 8 2
  – 1 5 9 5
  ─────────

  ─────────
```

3 Complete the missing answers in these number spiders.

a)

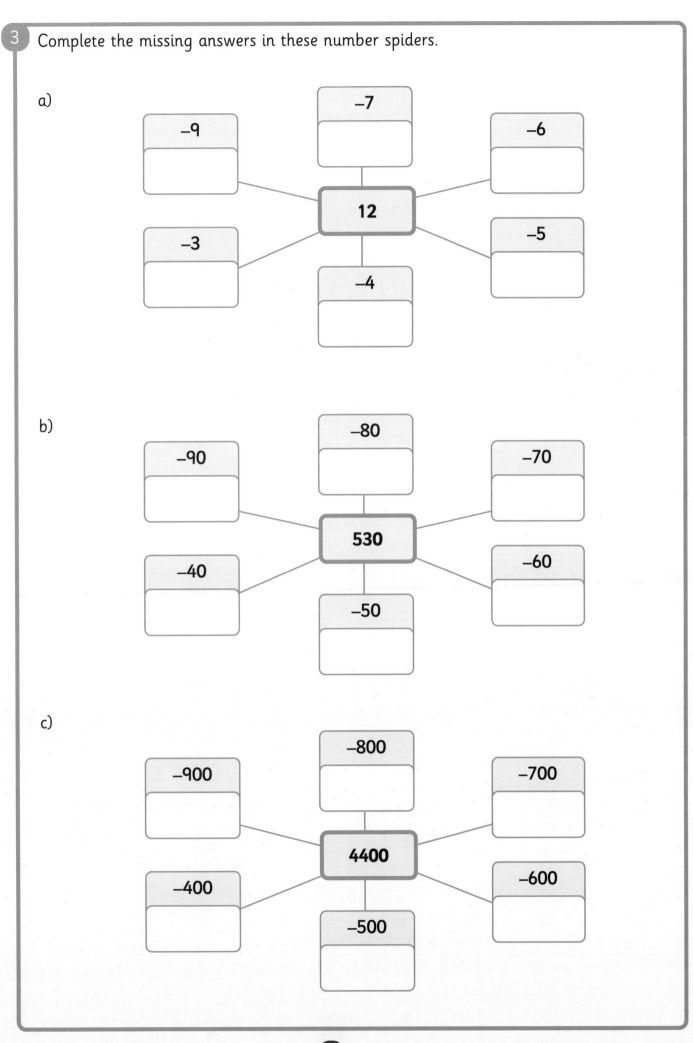

−9

−7

−6

12

−3

−5

−4

b)

−80

−90

−70

530

−40

−60

−50

c)

−800

−900

−700

4400

−400

−600

−500

4 Complete the calculations and complete the puzzle.

	1			2	3	4	
				5			
	6	7					8
	9					10	
		11					
	12						

Across

2.
$$\begin{array}{r} 3628 \\ -\ 1714 \\ \hline \end{array}$$

5.
$$\begin{array}{r} 4365 \\ -\ 3644 \\ \hline \end{array}$$

6.
$$\begin{array}{r} 4529 \\ -\ 2901 \\ \hline \end{array}$$

9.
$$\begin{array}{r} 5637 \\ -\ 5595 \\ \hline \end{array}$$

10.
$$\begin{array}{r} 1360 \\ -\ 1279 \\ \hline \end{array}$$

11.
$$\begin{array}{r} 7064 \\ -\ 6173 \\ \hline \end{array}$$

12.
$$\begin{array}{r} 5066 \\ -\ 1039 \\ \hline \end{array}$$

Down

1.
$$\begin{array}{r} 8228 \\ -\ 1714 \\ \hline \end{array}$$

2.
$$\begin{array}{r} 6944 \\ -\ 6772 \\ \hline \end{array}$$

3.
$$\begin{array}{r} 9039 \\ -\ 8111 \\ \hline \end{array}$$

4.
$$\begin{array}{r} 8002 \\ -\ 7991 \\ \hline \end{array}$$

7.
$$\begin{array}{r} 8198 \\ -\ 1908 \\ \hline \end{array}$$

8.
$$\begin{array}{r} 6509 \\ -\ 2343 \\ \hline \end{array}$$

Create 4 subtraction calculations so that the puzzle is correct.

^{1}4			
^{2}3	2	^{3}6	
8		3	
^{4}2	7	8	2

Across

2.

4.

Down

1.

3.

1 Use a standard algorithm to work these out.

a)
```
  3 6 6
- 1 2 7
-------
```

b)
```
  3 6 6
- 1 2 9
-------
```

c)
```
  3 9 6
- 1 2 8
-------
```

d)
```
  3 9 6
- 1 4 7
-------
```

e)
```
  5 7 4
- 2 4 5
-------
```

f)
```
  5 7 6
- 2 4 8
-------
```

g)
```
  5 7 8
- 3 4 9
-------
```

h)
```
  5 8 0
- 3 4 9
-------
```

2 Use a standard algorithm to work these out.

a)
```
  8 2 7
- 5 5 5
-------
```

b)
```
  8 2 7
- 4 4 4
-------
```

c)
```
  8 2 7
- 3 3 3
-------
```

d)
```
  8 0 3
- 3 3 3
-------
```

e)
```
  9 4 9
- 4 9 7
-------
```

f)
```
  9 4 9
- 4 8 7
-------
```

g)
```
  9 4 9
- 4 5 8
-------
```

h)
```
  9 3 9
- 4 5 8
-------
```

3 Use a standard algorithm to work these out.

a)
```
  7 1 3
- 5 2 5
-------
```

b)
```
  7 1 3
- 5 3 5
-------
```

c)
```
  7 1 3
- 5 4 6
-------
```

d)
```
  7 0 3
- 5 4 6
-------
```

e)
```
  6 6 3
- 2 7 7
-------
```

f)
```
  6 5 3
- 2 7 7
-------
```

g)
```
  6 4 3
- 2 8 7
-------
```

h)
```
  6 3 3
- 2 9 7
-------
```

0	1	2	3	4	5

1) Use the digits 0 to 5 to create calculations where you have to exchange twice.
Find the answers to your calculations.

☐☐☐☐   ☐☐☐☐   ☐☐☐☐
- ☐☐☐☐   - ☐☐☐☐   - ☐☐☐☐
_____   _____   _____

_____   _____   _____

2) Create three subtraction questions where the answer is always 5555.
The first question should have no exchange, the second 1 exchange and the third 2 exchanges.

☐☐☐☐   ☐☐☐☐   ☐☐☐☐
- ☐☐☐☐   - ☐☐☐☐   - ☐☐☐☐
_____   _____   _____

_____   _____   _____

3.9 Subtracting four-digit numbers using standard algorithms

1 Write the number shown here.

3 hundreds	40 ones	

3 hundreds	4 tens	

3 hundreds	40 tens	

3 hundreds	4 tens	4 ones	

3 hundreds	4 tens	40 ones	

3 hundreds	40 tens	40 ones	

2 Find the incorrect calculations. Draw a ring around them.

a)
```
  3 1 2 1
  4 7 3 4
- 1 9 2 7
---------
  2 8 0 7
```

b)
```
  3 1 2 1
  4 8 3 4
- 2 9 2 7
---------
  1 7 0 7
```

c)
```
      1 1
  4 6 2 3
- 1 7 1 4
---------
  3 1 0 9
```

d)
```
  3 1
  4 0 2 3
- 1 7 1 2
---------
  2 3 1 1
```

3. Calculate these:

a)
```
  5 3 1 6
- 2 4 7 2
---------
```

b)
```
  5 3 0 6
- 2 5 7 2
---------
```

c)
```
  6 3 0 5
- 3 5 8 8
---------
```

d)
```
  6 3 1 5
- 3 5 8 8
---------
```

e)
```
  8 0 1 2
- 3 4 1 1
---------
```

f)
```
  8 1 0 2
- 3 4 1 1
---------
```

g)
```
  8 1 2 0
- 3 4 1 1
---------
```

h)
```
  8 0 0 2
- 3 4 1 1
---------
```

★ **Challenge**

Fill in the missing digits to make each subtraction correct.

1.
```
  ☐ 8 ☐ 7
- 4 ☐ 1 ☐
---------
  1 9 1 9
```

2.
```
    5 7 3 7
- ☐ ☐ ☐ ☐
---------
  1 9 1 9
```

3.10 Mental and written strategies

1 Using these methods, solve this calculation **1569 + 546**.

a) An empty number line.

|————————————————————————————————————|

1569

b) Partitioning.

_____ + _____ + _____ + _____ + _____ + _____

c) Column partitioning.

```
  1 5 6 9
+   5 4 6
```

d) Standard algorithm

```
  1 5 6 9
+   5 4 6
```

2 Use the cards to create three addition calculations that are most efficiently solved as mental calculations.

3600   3876   5397

2040   2667   1199

_____ + _____ = _____

_____ + _____ = _____

_____ + _____ = _____

3

	Distance in kilometres
Inverness to Aberdeen	166
Edinburgh to Glasgow	75
Glasgow to Inverness	270
Dundee to Edinburgh	100
Aberdeen to Dundee	106

How far is it to get from Inverness to Glasgow, passing through Aberdeen, Dundee and Edinburgh?

Write down your method.

★ Challenge

Finlay adds two four-digit numbers to make a total of 11074. He only uses the digits 3 and 7.

a) What are his two numbers?

☐☐☐☐

+ ☐☐☐☐

b) If Finlay created a subtraction using his two numbers, what would the answer be?

3.11 Representing and solving word problems

1 One of these bar models is incorrect. Put a cross beside the incorrect representations.

a) Nuria spent £1.25 on chocolate and £7.50 on a cinema ticket.
How much did she spend altogether?

£1.25	£7.50

b) Finlay spent two hours at the leisure centre. He played in the ball pit for 45 minutes. How long did he spend in the rest of the centre?

120 minutes	
45 minutes	

c) Amman is 156cm tall. When he was five years old, he was 120 cm.
How much has he grown since he was five?

120 cm	156 cm

d) Isla has read 178 pages of her library book. She still has 189 pages to go.
How many pages does her book have?

178	189

2 Complete each Think Board.

Word problem	Bar model
Isla's gran was born in 1963. How old is she this year?	

Answer

Empty number line	Calculation

Word problem	Bar model
	455 | 545

Answer

Empty number line	Calculation

Word problem	Bar model

Answer

Empty number line	Calculation
	$$\begin{array}{r} {\scriptstyle 1\ 1} \\ 6\,9\,4\,1 \\ +\ 1\,7\,7\,7 \\ \hline 8\,7\,1\,8 \end{array}$$

⭐ **Challenge**

The local theatre has seats for 3059 people. At the beginning of June there are 1184 seats left for the Summer Show. By the middle of July another 543 tickets have been sold. How many free tickets are still available? Draw a bar model to show your thinking.

3.12 Solving multi-step word problems

1. The school fair hopes to raise £3000 for a new climbing frame.

   The raffle raises £1200 and the café raises half this amount.

   How much more do they need to raise to have enough money?

2. The school library has 9897 books on the shelves.

   The librarian puts 189 damaged books in the paper recycling bin.

   The teachers get a donation of 165 books from the local book shop.

   How many books does the library have now?

3. Isla's sister starts a new job. She works every Monday, Tuesday, Thursday and Friday.

   She is paid £1300 after her first month. She paid £275 for her train fares to work and £67 for lunches. She wants to buy a second-hand motorbike, which costs £1099. Is this possible? Explain your thinking.

4 The local football club has space for 8867 people. At the Saturday match there are 468 unsold tickets. There are 2041 children at the game.

How many adults are at the game?

5 Amman scored 1644 points playing his computer game.

Nuria scored 2374 more than Amman and Finlay beat both of them by scoring 709 more points than Nuria.

How many points did Finlay score?

6 Isla, her five-year-old sister and her mum and dad are looking forward to a family holiday.

The flights are £465 for adults and £325 for children.

The hotel is £1850 for a week.

How much will the trip cost?

7 Amman's uncle has walked 132 miles to raise money for charity.

He still has 248 miles to go until the finish point.

How far does he still need to walk before he is halfway there?

8 In January, the supermarket sells 8076 eggs. In February, it sells half that amount.

How many eggs are sold over the two months?

★ **Challenge**

On Monday the baker bakes 242 chocolate muffins, 164 cupcakes and 34 fruitcakes.

She sells three quarters of the goods in the bakery shop and donates a quarter to the local bowling club.

How many cakes does the bowling club get?

3.13 Adding decimal fractions and whole numbers

1 Round and adjust these calculations. The first one has been done for you.

a) $6 \cdot 5 + 99 = 5 \cdot 5 + 100$

b) $8 \cdot 5 + 199 = $

c) $9 \cdot 3 + 149 = $

d) $149 + 19 \cdot 3 = $

e) $148 + 29 \cdot 3 = $

f) $31 \cdot 9 + 5 \cdot 4 = $

g) $31 \cdot 8 + 5 \cdot 4 = $

h) $31 \cdot 5 + 5 \cdot 7 = $

2 Use partitions to solve these calculations. The first one has been done for you.

a) $62 \cdot 3 + 3 \cdot 6 = 60 + 2 + 3 + 0 \cdot 3 + 0 \cdot 6 = 65 + 0 \cdot 9 = 65 \cdot 9$

b) $72 \cdot 3 + 3 \cdot 6 = $

c) 72·4 + 4·6 =

d) 72·4 + 14·6 =

e) 78·4 + 14·8 =

f) 78·5 + 24·5 =

g) 88·5 + 24·6 =

3 Use a strategy of your choice to solve these calculations.

a) 8·8 + 4·4 =

b) 18·8 + 14·4 =

c) 20·4 + 4·9 =

d) 24·9 + 7·7 =

e) 24·8 + 6·7 =

f) 14·7 + 12·3 =

g) 14·3 + 12·7 =

4·7   13·9

12·6   7·4   4·9

12·8   6·5

Choose two numbers to create an addition where round and adjust is a good strategy. Solve your problem. Now choose two different numbers and solve by partitioning. You can use each number only once.

Round and adjust

Partitioning

1 Complete the table. The first one is done for you.

Decimal fractions < 1	Ones	Tenths	Number
0·6 + 0·6	1	2	1·2
0·6 + 0·8			1·4
0·8 + 0·7			
0·8 +	1	6	
+ 0·7	1	4	
0·9 +		8	

2 Use a number line to find the answers.

a) 23·5 + ☐ = 40

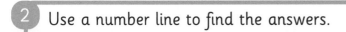

23·5   40

b) 23·7 + ☐ = 50

23·7   50

c) 33·7 + ☐ = 60

33·7   60

d) $60 = $ [ ] $+ 33.1$

```
├──────────────────────────────────────────────┤
33·1                                            60
```

e) $60 = $ [ ] $+ 43.2$

```
├──────────────────────────────────────────────┤
43·2                                            60
```

f) $73.2 + $ [ ] $= 100$

```
├──────────────────────────────────────────────┤
73·2                                           100
```

3 Find the missing number in each bar model.

a)

50	
13·9	

b)

55	
21·9	

c)

21·9	38·1

d)

46·6	34·4

★ Challenge

1. Complete the magic square using the numbers 0·2, 0·3, 0·5. 0·7 and 0·8. Each row, column and diagonal must have the same total.

		0·6
0·4	0·9	

2. Experiment with making your own magic square with decimal fractions!

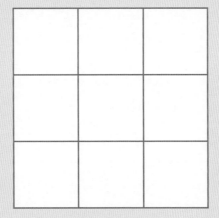

69

1 Double these numbers:

a) Double 6 = [ ]

b) Double 9 = [ ]

c) Double 12 = [ ]

d) Double 15 = [ ]

e) Double 18 = [ ]

f) Double 21 = [ ]

g) Double 24 = [ ]

h) Double 27 = [ ]

i) Double 30 = [ ]

j) Double 33 = [ ]

2 Calculate these by using your knowledge of the 3 times table and doubling. The first one has been done for you.

a) $3 \times 2 =$ [6]

b) $3 \times 4 =$ [ ]

c) $3 \times 6 =$ [ ]

$6 \times 2 =$ [12]

$6 \times 4 =$ [ ]

$6 \times 6 =$ [ ]

d) $3 \times 8 =$ [ ]

e) $3 \times 10 =$ [ ]

f) $3 \times 5 =$ [ ]

$6 \times 8 =$ [ ]

$6 \times 10 =$ [ ]

$6 \times 5 =$ [ ]

3 Complete the fact families. One has been done for you.

a)
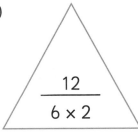

b)
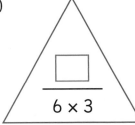

c)
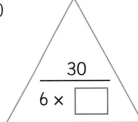

d)
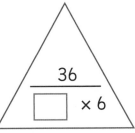

e)
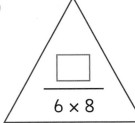

f)
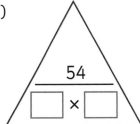

★ Challenge

Write the fact families for 6 up to 6 × 10.

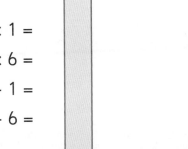

6 × 1 =
1 × 6 =
6 ÷ 1 =
6 ÷ 6 =

1 Calculate these by using your knowledge of the 10 times table. The first one has been done for you.

a)

$4 \times 9 = (4 \times 10) - (4 \times 1)$

$= 40 - 4$

$= 36$

b)

$8 \times 9 = ($ ⬚ $\times 10) - ($ ⬚ $\times 1)$

$=$ ⬚ $-$ ⬚

$=$ ⬚

2 Complete the following:

a) $9 \times 10 =$ [ ]

b) $45 \div 9 =$ [ ]

c) [ ] $\div 9 = 2$

d) $4 \times 9 =$ [ ]

e) $54 \div 9 =$ [ ]

f) [ ] $\div 9 = 8$

g) [ ] $\div 9 = 7$

h) $3 \times 9 =$ [ ]

i) $99 \div 9 =$ [ ]

j) [ ] $\div 9 = 1$

1. Complete the table.

	Tens	Ones
9 × 1	0	9
9 × 2		
9 × 3		
9 × 4		
9 × 5		
9 × 6		

2. Look at the pattern of your answers. What do you notice? Keep exploring – what is the first fact when this does not happen?

Use this box to explore the pattern.

4.3 Multiplying multiples of 10, 100 and 1000

1 Circle the facts that are incorrect and correct them. Now fill in the missing facts.

	× 10	× 100	× 1000
65		6500	
70	7000		
75			75 000
80			8000
85		850	
90	900		
95		9500	

2 Complete these calculations. The first one is done for you.

a) 4 × 30 = 4 × 3 tens

      = 12 tens

      = 120

b) 4 × 40 = 4 × ▢ tens

      = ▢ tens

      = ▢

c) 4 × 400 = 4 × ▢ hundreds

      = ▢ hundreds

      = ▢

d) 5 × 600 = 5 × ▢ hundreds

      = ▢ hundreds

      = ▢

3 Calculate the following:

a) 9×7 = [　　　]

90 × 7 = [　　　]

900 × 7 = [　　　]

9000 × 7 = [　　　]

b) 6×8 = [　　　]

60 × 8 = [　　　]

6000 × 8 = [　　　]

600 × 8 = [　　　]

c) Glendale Football Club charges £8 for a child ticket to see a match. They sell 600 child tickets. How much money do the make?

[　　　]

d) An adult ticket to see a match is £40. Isla's mum buys tickets for herself and six friends. How much does she pay?

[　　　]

e) The shirt factory uses seven buttons on each shirt. How many buttons do they need to make 4000 shirts?

[　　　]

Use your knowledge of multiplying by multiples of 10, 100 and 1000 to solve these.

1. The answer is 2400. What could the question be? How many different ways can you find?

2. The answer is 12 000. What could the question be? How many different ways can you find?

3. The answer is 420. What could the question be? How many different ways can you find?

1 Complete the table.

	÷ 10	÷ 100	÷ 1000
6000			
8000			
2000			
5000			

2 Complete these calculations. The first one is done for you.

a) 160 ÷ 8 = 16 tens ÷ 8

= 2 tens

= 20

b) 240 ÷ 8 = ⬚ tens ÷ 8

= ⬚ tens

= ⬚

c) 3200 ÷ 8 = ⬚ hundreds ÷ 8

= ⬚ hundreds

= ⬚

d) 3200 ÷ 4 = ⬚ hundreds ÷ 4

= ⬚ hundreds

= ⬚

e) $32\,000 \div 4 = \boxed{}$ thousands ÷ 4   f) $36\,000 \div 4 = \boxed{}$ thousands ÷ 4

$= \boxed{}$ thousands $= \boxed{}$ thousands

$= \boxed{}$ $= \boxed{}$

---

3 Use these known facts to help you.

| $49 \div 7 = 7$ | $36 \div 6 = 6$ | $25 \div 5 = 5$ | $16 \div 4 = 4$ |

a) $4900 \div 7 = \boxed{}$ b) $250 \div 5 = \boxed{}$ c) $36\,000 \div 6 = \boxed{}$

d) $1600 \div 4 = \boxed{}$ e) $160 \div 4 = \boxed{}$ f) $3600 \div 6 = \boxed{}$

g) $490 \div 7 = \boxed{}$ h) $25\,000 \div 5 = \boxed{}$ i) $2500 \div 5 = \boxed{}$

---

4 Solve the following:

a) Apples are sold in bags of five. The school cook orders 4500 apples.
   How many bags does she order?

b) Bananas are sold in bunches of six bananas. The school cook orders 540 bananas. How many bunches does she order?

c) Oranges are sold in bags of four. The school cook orders 3600 oranges. How many bags does she order?

★ Challenge

Fill in the blanks using the digits 0, 2 and 4. You can use each digit as often as you like. All numbers must be multiples of 10, 100 or 1000.

☐☐☐ ÷ ☐☐ = ☐

☐☐☐☐ ÷ ☐☐ = ☐

☐☐☐☐☐ ÷ ☐☐ = ☐

4.5 Solving division problems

1

Solve the following calcuations. Use the dots above to help you.

a) 3 × 5 = [ ]

b) [ ] × 3 = 15

c) [ ] ÷ 5 = 3

d) 15 ÷ [ ] = 5

2 Complete the following calculations. The first has been done for you.

a) What is 18 divided by 2? [9] × 2 = 18 so 18 ÷ 2 = [9]

b) What is 18 divided by 3? [ ] × 3 = 18 so 18 ÷ 3 = [ ]

c) What is 18 divided by 9? [ ] × 9 = 18 so 18 ÷ 9 = [ ]

d) What is 36 divided by 9? [ ] × 9 = 36 so 36 ÷ 9 = [ ]

e) What is 36 divided by 6? [ ] × 6 = 36 so 36 ÷ 6 = [ ]

f) What is 36 divided by 4? [ ] × 4 = 36 so 36 ÷ 4 = [ ]

g) What is 36 divided by 3? [ ] × 3 = 36 so 36 ÷ 3 = [ ]

3 Complete the following by writing x or ÷ in each box. The first has been done for you.

a) 12 | × | 2 = 24

b) 24 | ☐ | 2 = 12

c) 24 | ☐ | 12 = 2

d) 2 | ☐ | 12 = 24

e) 24 | ☐ | 3 = 8

f) 8 | ☐ | 3 = 24

g) 4 | ☐ | 6 = 24

h) 24 | ☐ | 6 = 4

4 Use the inverse relationship between multiplication and division to solve these.

a) £50 is shared between two brothers.
How much does each brother get?

b) 50 pencils are shared between ten children.
How many does each child get?

c) 100 books are shared equally between ten classes.
How many does each class get?

d) 25 milk cartons are shared equally between five groups.
How many does each group get?

e) 45 lemons are shared equally between five school cooks.
How many does each cook get?

f) £45 is shared equally between nine children.
How much does each child get?

1) Use these facts to answer the following:

16 × 7 = 112

362 × 14 = 5068

452 ÷ 113 = 4

a) 112 ÷ 7 = ☐

b) 14 × ☐ = 5068

c) 452 ÷ ☐ = 113

d) 7 × 16 = ☐

e) 5068 ÷ 362 = ☐

f) 14 × ☐ = 5068

g) 112 ÷ 16 = ☐

h) 4 × ☐ = 452

2) Now create three calculations using the facts above.

4.6 Solving multiplication problems

1 Partition these numbers by place value. The first one is one for you.

a) 36 = 30 + 6

b) 26 =

c) 28 =

d) 58 =

e) 158 =

f) 142 =

2 Use the grids to answer the following:

a) 132 × 4

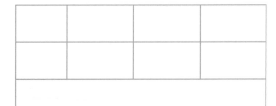

b) 138 × 4

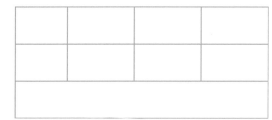

c) 138 × 5

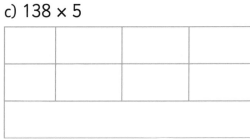

d) 238 × 6

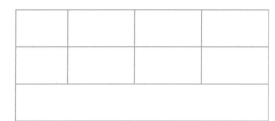

3 Find the answers. Draw grids to show your calculations.

a) Mr Green earned £424 per week for four weeks. How much did he earn during that time?

b) Mrs Lemon got a delivery of sweets for her shop. She got eight boxes with 164 chocolate bars in each. How many bars of chocolate did she get?

c) Ms Brown put £8·45 in her new piggy bank each week for nine weeks. How much did she have in it at the end of nine weeks?

★ Challenge

- Make three different numbers using the digits 3, 6 and 9.
- Ask a friend to choose a number between 2 and 9 for you to multiply your numbers by.

Use multiplication grids to help you find the answers.

1.

2.

3.

1 Match the number to the partition.

56	60 + 21
81	33 + 33
66	60 + 33
48	40 + 16
93	24 + 24

2 Use the partitions in question 1 to complete these division calculations. Complete the grids. The first one is done for you.

a) 56 ÷ 4

÷	40	16
4	10	4
10 + 4 = 14		

b) 81 ÷ 3

÷	60	21
3		
+ =		

c) 66 ÷ 3

÷	33	33
3		
+ =		

d) 48 ÷ 6

÷		
6		
+ =		

e) 93 ÷ 3

÷		
+ =		

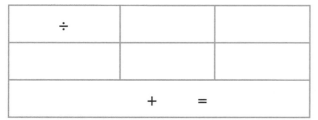

3 Use the partition method to solve these problems.

There are 132 children in Glenwood School. How many groups will be needed if there are:

a) three children in each group?

b) four children in each group?

c) six children in each group?

★ **Challenge**

1. Use different partitions to show 168 ÷ 4.

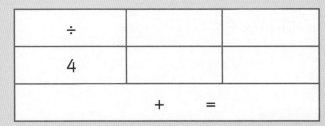

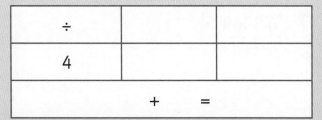

	÷		
	4		
	+	=	

	÷		
	4		
	+	=	

	÷		
	4		
	+	=	

	÷		
	4		
	+	=	

2. Which partition did you find worked best? Why might that be?

1

a) Use the diagram to show how 20 × 4 can help you answer 19 × 4.

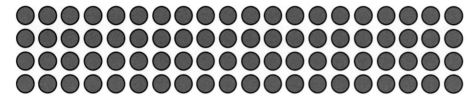

19 × 4 = [ ]

b) Use the ten frames to show 9 × 9 using compensation.

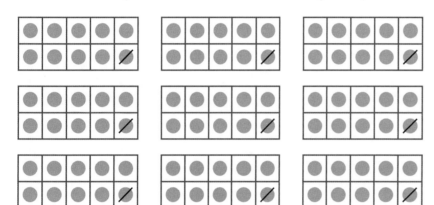

9 × 10 = [ ] [ ] − 9 = 81

So 9 × 9 = [ ]

c) Draw ten frames or use a set of ten frames to help you solve these:

   i) 3 × 9   ii) 11 × 9

2 Use the number line to show:

a) 19 × 4 = [ ]

|———————————————————————————————
0

b) 18 × 4 = [ ]

|———————————————————————————————
0

3 Use rounding and compensation to help you solve these problems:

a) 5 × 40 = 200 so 5 × 39 = [ ]   5 × 41 = [ ]

b) 6 × 40 = 240 so 6 × 39 = [ ]   6 × 38 = [ ]

★ Challenge

| 0 | 1 | 2 | 3 | 4 | 5 |

Amman used two of these digits to create a number. He multiplied his two-digit number by one of the remaining digits and got an answer of 120.

1. What was Amman's two-digit number?

2. What did he multiply his two-digit number by?

[ ]

4.9 Solving problems involving addition, subtraction, multiplication and division

1. Amman says that he can solve 36 × 4 by adding.
Finlay says that is not possible. Who is correct and why?

2. Edinburgh is 648km from London, Cardiff is 240km from London and Belfast is 742km from London. Mr Wood and Ms Stone are lorry drivers.

   a) Mr Wood drives from Edinburgh to London and back again twice in July. How far does he travel?

   b) Ms Stone drives from Cardiff to London and back three times in July. Who drove further in July and by how much?

3 The supermarket has a deal on fruit. Lemons, oranges and limes are £2 for a bag of six or they can be bought for 35p each. Apples cost 40p each or £3 for a bag of six.

a) Amman's mum buys 36 lemons. What is the least she has to pay?

b) Amman's dad buys 12 apples. What is the least he has to pay?

c) Amman's grandad buys three bags of limes and three bags of apples. How much does he pay?

4 Four children are selling cookies they have made. They sell them for 50p each. How much will they each get if they sell:

a) 124 cookies at school?

b) 96 cookies at the local library?

c) 280 cookies at the village show?

d) How much money do the children make altogether?

5 Mr Young has been offered two jobs.

- The pet shop pays £12 each hour and he would work 36 hours each week.
- The garage pays £14 each hour and he would work 32 hours each week.

Which job would pay the most?

Challenge

Nuria's birthday treat is a visit to the cinema. She is going with her mum, her aunt, her uncle and her three cousins.

What is the cheapest way they can get tickets?

Remember to show your working.

CINEMA

Adult: £11
Child: £7
Family: £30 (2 adults, 2 children)

4.10 Multiplying decimal fractions

1 Complete these calculations. The first one is done for you.

a) [4] × 3 = 12

b) [   ] × 3 = 120

c) [   ] × 3 = 1200

d) [   ] × 3 = 12 000

e) [   ] × 6 = 24

f) [   ] × 6 = 240

g) 400 × [   ] = 2400

h) 4000 × [   ] = 24 000

2 Record your answers in the table. The first one has been done for you.

	Thousands	Hundreds	Tens	Ones		Tenths
a) 0·6				0	·	6
b) 0·6 × 10					·	
c) 0·6 × 100					·	
d) 0·6 × 1000					·	

3 Multiply these decimals and record the answer on the grid.

a)

Tens	Ones	Decimal point	Tenths
	0	·	1

 × 10

Tens	Ones	Decimal point	Tenths
		·	

b)

Tens	Ones	Decimal point	Tenths
	0	·	3

 × 10

Tens	Ones	Decimal point	Tenths
		·	

c)

Tens	Ones	Decimal point	Tenths
	1	.	3

 × 10

Tens	Ones	Decimal point	Tenths
		.	

d)

Tens	Ones	Decimal point	Tenths
	2	.	3

 × 10

Tens	Ones	Decimal point	Tenths
		.	

---

4 Multiply these decimals and record the answer on the grid.

a)

Tens	Ones	Decimal point	Tenths
	0	.	1

× 100

Tens	Ones	Decimal point	Tenths
		.	

b)

Tens	Ones	Decimal point	Tenths
	0	.	3

 × 100

Tens	Ones	Decimal point	Tenths
		.	

c)

Tens	Ones	Decimal point	Tenths
	1	.	3

 × 100

Tens	Ones	Decimal point	Tenths
		.	

d)

Tens	Ones	Decimal point	Tenths
	2	.	3

 × 100

Tens	Ones	Decimal point	Tenths
		.	

5 Multiply these decimals.

a) 1·7 × 10 = [ ]

b) 1·7 × 100 = [ ]

c) 1·7 × 1000 = [ ]

d) 3·7 × 10 = [ ]

e) 4·7 × [ ] = 470

f) 5·7 × [ ] = 5700

g) [ ] × 10 = 53

h) [ ] × 100 = 53

6 There are 1000g in a kg. How many grams are there in:

a) 2kg = [ ]

b) 2·5kg = [ ]

c) 2·25kg = [ ]

d) 2·75kg = [ ]

e) 0·75kg = [ ]

f) 0·66kg = [ ]

g) 5·66kg = [ ]

h) 12·66kg = [ ]

★ Challenge

Amman's answer is 5700. What might his question be?

Use just the cards below to show as many questions as possible.

[ ]

(0·57) (57) (0·057)

(570) (5·7) (5700)

× 10   × 100   × 1000

4.11 Dividing whole numbers by 10, 100 and 1000

1 Decide whether these calculations are correct or incorrect. Use ✔ or ✘.

a) 720 ÷ 10 = 72

b) 7200 ÷ 100 = 720

c) 72 000 ÷ 1000 = 72

d) 72 000 ÷ 10 = 720

2 Divide these numbers and record the answers on the grids.

a)

Hundreds	Tens	Ones
	4	5

 ÷ 10

Tens	Ones	Decimal point	Tenths
		.	

b)

Hundreds	Tens	Ones
4	5	0

 ÷ 10

Tens	Ones	Decimal point	Tenths
		.	

c)

Hundreds	Tens	Ones
4	5	5

 ÷ 10

Tens	Ones	Decimal point	Tenths
		.	

d)

Hundreds	Tens	Ones
4	0	5

÷ 10

Tens	Ones	Decimal point	Tenths
		.	

3 Divide these numbers and record the answers on the grids.

a)

Thousands	Hundreds	Tens	Ones
1	7	6	0

÷ 100

Tens	Ones	Decimal point	Tenths
		.	

b)

Thousands	Hundreds	Tens	Ones
1	7	1	0

÷ 1000 →

Tens	Ones	Decimal point	Tenths
		.	

c)

Thousands	Hundreds	Tens	Ones
1	7	6	0

÷ 1000 →

Tens	Ones	Decimal point	Tenths
		.	

d)

Thousands	Hundreds	Tens	Ones
		1	7

÷ 100 →

Tens	Ones	Decimal point	Tenths
		.	

---

4 Divide these numbers.

a) 96 ÷ 10 = ☐   b) 96 ÷ 100 = ☐

c) 9 ÷ 100 = ☐   d) 90 ÷ 1000 = ☐

e) 900 ÷ ☐ = 0·9   f) 9 ÷ ☐ = 0·9

g) ☐ ÷ 10 = 0·7   h) ☐ ÷ 100 = 0·7

---

5 There are 100cm in a metre. Convert these cm to m.

a) 560cm = ☐   b) 56cm = ☐

c) 5600cm = ☐   d) 725cm = ☐

e) 775cm = ☐   f) 750cm = ☐

★ Challenge

1. Using the cards shown below, create ten different number sentences.

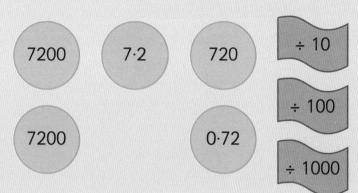

7200   7·2   720   ÷ 10

÷ 100

7200   0·72   ÷ 1000

2. Now find the answers to the questions you created.

For example:

7200 ÷ 100 = 72

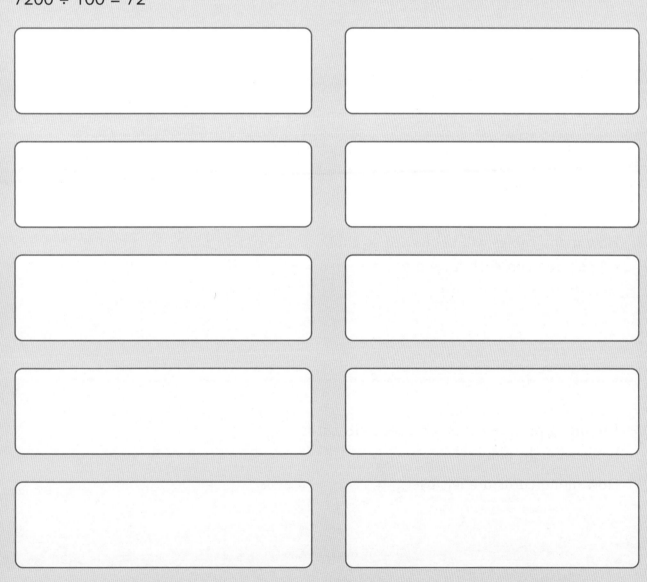

1. Order these numbers from smallest to biggest.

0·3 $\frac{4}{8}$ 5·2   0·25

2. Amman's teacher sorts the 30 children in the class into four teams for a game of football.

How many children are left without a team?

3. The dinner tables in the school hall each sit six people.

How many tables will be needed so that 64 children can each have a seat?

4. Isla has a pack of cards. She deals 38 cards between eight players.

How many cards are left over?

5 Granny gives Nuria and her sister £13 to share.

How much do they each get?

6 Ms Brown goes to the café with her three friends.
The bill comes to £26 and they all pay the
same amount.

How much does each person pay?

7 Finlay is saving up for a new toy. It costs £32·50
and he saves the same amount each week.
After five weeks he has saved exactly £32·50.

How much did he save each week?

8 Mrs Black bakes three cakes which she shares
between her two sisters.

How many cakes does each sister get?

9 Mrs Wood bakes 21 muffins which she shares between her six children.

How many muffins does each child get?

10 Amman takes the bus to see his Gran. The bus travels six miles and takes 45 minutes.

How long does it take to travel one mile?

★ Challenge

Which question best matches which answer?   **5·75**   **5 $\frac{3}{4}$**   **5 remainder 3**

1. Bob has baked 23 cookies which he sells in bags of four. How many bags will he fill?

2. Bob spent £23 on four copies of a book for himself and his three friends. How much was each book?

3. Bob ran four races over the weekend. It took him 23 hours in total and each race took him the same length of time. How long did each race take?

4.13 Solving multiplication and division problems

Complete these Think Boards.

1

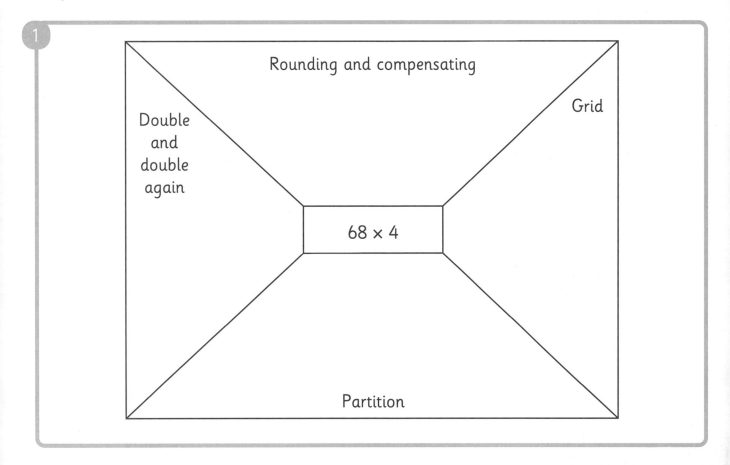

Rounding and compensating

Double and double again

Grid

68 × 4

Partition

2

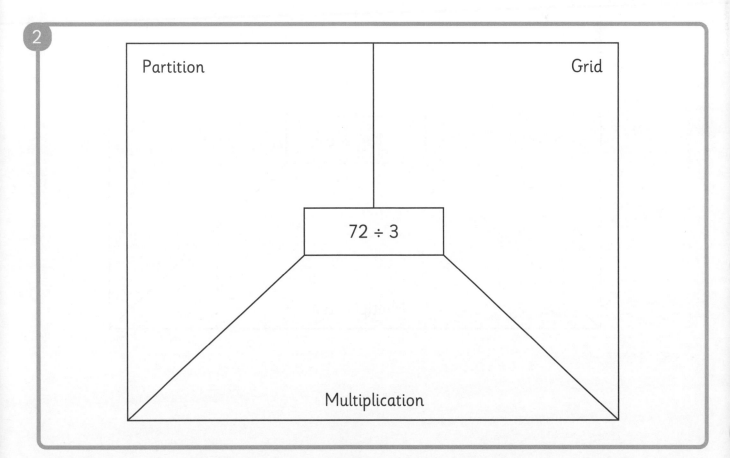

Partition

Grid

72 ÷ 3

Multiplication

3

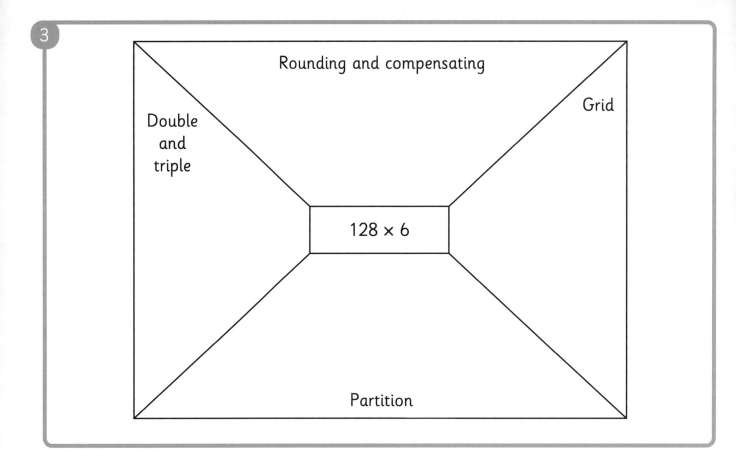

Rounding and compensating

Grid

Double
and
triple

128 × 6

Partition

4

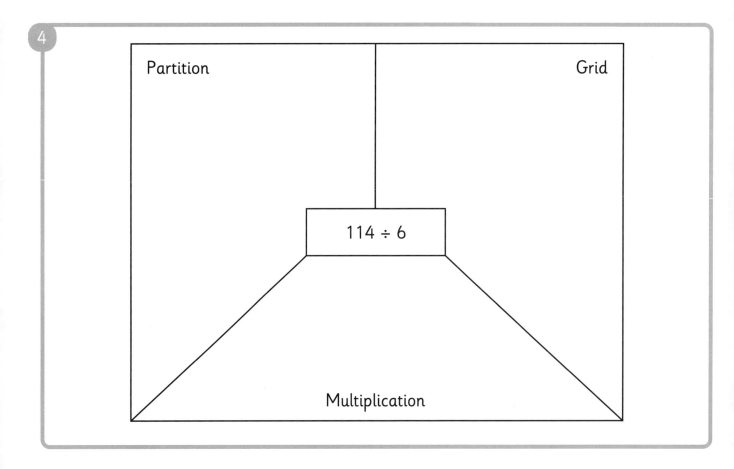

Partition

Grid

114 ÷ 6

Multiplication

Nuria has a great magic trick which means she ALWAYS knows the answer. Finlay doesn't believe Nuria's trick will always works. What do you think?

Try Nuria's trick for different numbers. Compare your findings with a friend. Who is correct, Nuria or Finlay?

a) Write down any number.

b) Add 5 to your number.

c) Multiply this new number by 3.

d) Now subtract 15.

e) Divide your answer by the number you first thought of.

f) Next add 7.

g) The answer is ...

Attempt 1

Attempt 2

Attempt 3

Attempt 4

Attempt 5

Who is correct?

5.1 Identifying all factors of a number

1 Complete the Venn diagram.

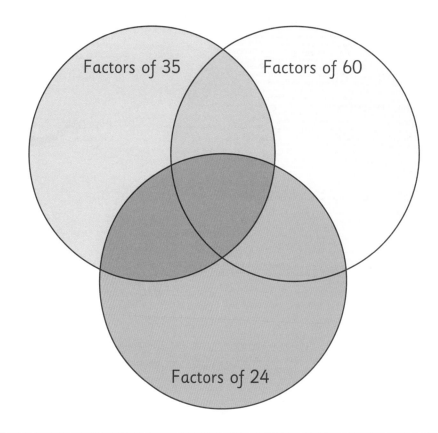

Factors of 35

Factors of 60

Factors of 24

2 Use the numbers 1 to 30. You can use each number only once. Find a number that has:

a) an odd number as a factor

b) a factor greater than 14

c) an even number as a factor

d) only three factors

e) a factor that is less than 3

f) only two factors

3 a) Roll a dice. Which numbers less than 35 have your number as a factor?

Repeat this activity five times.

b) Use two dice and total them. Which numbers less than 110 have your number as a factor? Repeat this activity five times.

★ Challenge

I am a number between 1 and 45 and I have only eight factors.

Which number might I be?

5.2 Identifying multiples of numbers

1

1	2	3	4	5	6	7	8	9	10
11	12	13	14	15	16	17	18	19	20
21	22	23	24	25	26	27	28	29	30
31	32	33	34	35	36	37	38	39	40
41	42	43	44	45	46	47	48	49	50
51	52	53	54	55	56	57	58	59	60
61	62	63	64	65	66	67	68	69	70
71	72	73	74	75	76	77	78	79	80
81	82	83	84	85	86	87	88	89	90
91	92	93	94	95	96	97	98	99	100

a) Colour all the multiples of 10 yellow.

b) Colour all the multiples of 3 blue.

c) Colour all the multiples of 7 red.

d) Which numbers have you coloured in yellow and blue?

e) Which numbers have you coloured in blue and red?

f) Which number have you coloured in yellow and red?

2 Write these numbers in the correct place in the diagram.

Use numbers 12, 25, 40, 15, 9, 17, 6, 21, 16, 330.

(12) (17)

(25) (6)

(40) (21)

(15) (16)

(9) (330)

	Multiple of 5	Not multiple of 5
Multiple of 2		
Not multiple of 2		

3

	Multiple of 6	Multiple of 9	Neither a factor nor a multiple of 6 or 9
81		✔	
18			
108			
80			
1			
9			
91			
24			
48			

Find the lowest common multiple of these pairs. Have a multiplication square handy!

	Lowest Common Multiple	
3		4
3		5
3		6
6		9
5		9
4		9
3		9

Multiples of 3

Multiples of 4

Multiples of 5

Multiples of 6

Multiples of 9